The Importance of Physical Activity and Exercise:
The Fitness Factor

Obesity: Modern-Day Epidemic

The Importance of Physical Activity and Exercise:
The Fitness Factor

by
Autumn Libal

Mason Crest Publishers
Philadelphia

Mason Crest Publishers Inc.
370 Reed Road, Broomall, Pennsylvania 19008
(866) MCP-BOOK (toll free)
www.masoncrest.com

13 12 11 10 09 08 07   10 9 8 7 6 5 4 3

Library of Congress Cataloging-in-Publication Data

Libal, Autumn.
  The importance of physical activity and exercise : the fitness factor / by
Autumn Libal.
     p. cm.
    ISBN 978-1-59084-945-3
    ISBN 978-1-59084-941-5 (series)
 1. Physical fitness—Health aspects—Juvenile literature. 2. Exercise—
Health aspects—Juvenile literature. 3. Obesity—Prevention—Juvenile lit-
erature. 4. Lifestyles—Health aspects—United States—Juvenile literature.
I. Title.
  RA781.L4925 2005
  613.7'1—dc22

Design by MK Bassett-Harvey.
Composition by Harding House Publishing Service, Vestal, New York.
www.hardinghousepages.com
Cover design by Benjamin Stewart.
www.hardinghousepages.com
Printed in the Hashemite Kingdom of Jordan.

Contents

Introduction

We as a society often reserve our harshest criticism for those conditions we understand the least. Such is the case with obesity. Obesity is a chronic and often-fatal disease that accounts for 400,000 deaths each year. It is second only to smoking as a cause of premature death in the United States. People suffering from obesity need understanding, support, and medical assistance. Yet what they often receive is scorn.

Today, children are the fastest growing segment of the obese population in the United States. This constitutes a public health crisis of enormous proportions. Living with childhood obesity affects self-esteem, employment, and attainment of higher education. But childhood obesity is much more than a social stigma. It has serious health consequences.

Childhood obesity increases the risk for poor health in adulthood and premature death. Depression, diabetes, asthma, gallstones, orthopedic diseases, and other obesity-related conditions are all on the rise in children. Recent estimates suggest that 30 to 50 percent of children born in 2000 will develop type 2 diabetes mellitus—a leading cause of preventable blindness, kidney failure, heart disease, stroke, and amputations. Obesity is undoubtedly the most pressing nutritional disorder among young people today.

This series is an excellent first step toward understanding the obesity crisis and profiling approaches for remedying it. If we are to reverse obesity's current trend, there must be family, community, and national objectives promoting healthy eating and exercise. As a nation, we must demand broad-based public-health initiatives to limit TV watching, curtail junk food advertising toward children, and promote physical activity. More than rhetoric, these need to be our rallying cry. Anything short of this will eventually fail, and within our lifetime obesity will become the leading cause of death in the United States if not in the world.

Victor F. Garcia, M.D.
Founder, Bariatric Surgery Center
Cincinnati Children's Hospital Medical Center
Professor of Pediatrics and Surgery
School of Medicine
University of Cincinnati

chapter 1

Battle of the Bulge

- America in Crisis

- A Strange Paradox

America in Crisis

If you live in the United States of America, you can likely call yourself one of the luckiest people on earth. While all over the world people labor from sunup to sundown to obtain only the most basic necessities, Americans as a people are awash in surplus: surplus goods and surplus time. Our society is filled with technological marvels, time-saving appliances, and convenience items that simplify nearly every aspect of our lives. At every turn we have machines, gadgets, and companies that do our work for us: cars that practically drive

themselves, eliminating the need for us to walk; televisions that entertain us, eliminating our need to play; and prepackaged foods to eat, eliminating our need to cook. And yet, in the midst of all this surplus and splendor, a life-threatening crisis is brewing.

In a post–9/11 world, the word crisis seems to be on everyone's lips. The popular *media* is filled with stories of war, terrorism, and threats to homeland security. As frightening as these things are, the average American today is at risk from a much more immediate threat. This threat doesn't come from terrorists or warlords; it comes from our very own bodies. The signs are everywhere: they're in the headlines of newspapers, the titles of best-selling books, the lead stories on the nightly news, and the bodies of people all around you. In America today, obesity—the state of being very overweight—is not simply a problem, it's an *epidemic*. Two out of every three American adults are overweight, and one out of three American adults is officially obese. The crisis is also spreading to young people like never before. One out of every six people between the ages of six and nineteen is also overweight, with an additional one out of six in danger of becoming overweight. Today, the United States is the most overweight nation in the world, and the numbers (along with our waistlines) are growing. Experts now fear that obesity is quickly becoming an American way of life.

A Strange Paradox

Americans certainly have not decided they want to be obese. In fact, each year Americans pour billions of dollars into trying to lose weight. We might be the heaviest people in the world, but we also spend the most money trying to slim down.

America's obesity epidemic is a strange *paradox*, because although America is now the heaviest nation on earth, it is also one

> *We might be the heaviest people in the world, but we also spend the most money trying to slim down.*

of the most image conscious. At the same time that Americans are suffering from ballooning weight, they are bombarded by images telling them to be impossibly beautiful and impossibly thin. Think about the people you see on television, in movies, and splashed on the covers of magazines. How many real-life people do you know who actually look like this? Probably no one. And yet, how much do you, your friends, or your family members *want* to look like this? Probably a lot. Each year Americans spend billions of their hard-earned dollars not trying to get healthy, but trying to look like the images in magazines.

So, if we as a society care so deeply about appearance and being thin, why does the obesity crisis keep looming larger? Clearly there are forces at work that encourage us to make unhealthy lifestyle choices, forces that sometimes make it nearly impossible to do anything else. We will talk more about some of these forces in later chapters, but part of the problem is that when it comes to losing weight, too many of us have the wrong goals. We may become so focused on looking a certain way that we forget our goal should be good health. We may begin to hate the way our bodies look so much (even when they look the way the average human body is meant to look) that we become frustrated, give up, and sabotage our own health.

If our goal shouldn't be to get thin or look like a supermodel, why should we be concerned about overweight and obesity? After all, if a person is happy and comfortable with her body, why should she care if a number on a scale

None of us needs to strive to look like a supermodel, but we should all strive to be as healthy as we can be.

says she weighs too much? On the one hand, it is extremely important for people to learn to accept and be happy with their bodies and to realize that no one's body is perfect. Only a tiny handful of people on this earth can look like supermodels, and it's ridiculous for the rest of us to feel bad about ourselves when we can't achieve these unattainable looks. On the other hand, the health risks of overweight and obesity are so numerous and serious that people should not ignore a weight issue if it arises. None of us needs to strive to look like a supermodel, but we should all strive to be as healthy as we can.

Although there are a number of factors behind America's bulging bodies, lack of exercise is one of the largest. Most of us tend to live busy, fast-paced lives. With school to attend, work to complete, friends to see, e-mail to read, a favorite television show to catch, and numerous other demands on our time, it's easy to forget about the basic things we should do for our bodies every day. At the heart of America's weight crisis is a general abandonment of a physically active lifestyle—the very foundation of good health.

The Supermodel Myth

In magazines, women are tall and thin with perfect skin; voluptuous breasts; and long, flowing hair. Men are tall and tan with bulging biceps and rock-hard abs. But who actually looks like this? You may think these models are simply blessed with rare genes. They probably are, but their beauty secrets go much further. They also have dieticians, personal trainers, makeup artists, and sometimes even use drugs to achieve their perfect bodies. Their job is to look good, so huge amounts of time and money are devoted to developing this image. Even with all of this help, however, these models will still never look as good walking down the street as they do on the covers of magazines. That's because their perfect physiques are not just the product of good genes, starvation, hard work, and talented artists. They are also photographed under special lights and carefully planned conditions. After the photograph is taken, it undergoes an elaborate design process including airbrushing and computer enhancement to elimi-nate any remaining "flaws" and to "improve" parts of the body. Like so much of what you will read inside that magazine, the picture on its cover is a work of fiction.

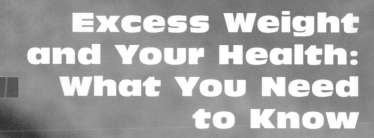

Chapter 2

Excess Weight and Your Health: What You Need to Know

- The Health Risks of Overweight and Obesity

- Understanding Overweight and Obesity

The Health Risks of Overweight and Obesity

Randy Clark, manager of the University of Wisconsin's Exercise Science Laboratory sees today's obesity epidemic as a matter of life and death. "This [generation of children]," he states, "is the first generation in history that will have a shorter life expectancy than that of their parents. Reduced activity, excess body fat, and excess body weight are important factors bringing about this sad fact." To some, Clark's views may sound *alarmist*. To others, it's just a matter of looking at the facts.

Today we are beginning to understand that the health risks of excess weight are far too serious to ignore. These risks include high cholesterol, high blood pressure, elevated *triglyceride* levels, heart disease, type 2 diabetes, *arthritis* and other *musculoskeletal* complications, numerous cancers, asthma and other breathing problems, decreased life expectancy, reproductive complications, and many more. Conditions like these carry risks and complications of their own. High cholesterol, high blood pressure, elevated triglyceride levels, and heart disease significantly increase one's risk of having a heart attack or stroke, which are often deadly. Type 2 diabetes, a disease characterized by the body's inability to regulate sugar levels in the blood, can lead to kidney damage, kidney failure, blindness, paralysis, limb amputation, and death. Arthritis, joint pain, and other complications of the musculoskeletal system, often brought on by the physical stress of supporting and carrying extra pounds, can lead to chronic discomfort and reduced mobility. Chronic pain and reduced mobility make it difficult to exercise and can thus compound one's weight issues. Cancer, of course, is another potentially deadly condition, and an increased risk of developing cancer of the colon, kidneys, gallbladder, prostate, uterus, breast, and other organs has been associated with excess weight.

Overweight and obesity, however, do not simply affect a person's physical health. They can also affect her mental health and social well-being. In our society, the majority of adults are overweight. Nevertheless, overweight and obesity continue to carry huge social *stigma*. Besides the numerous health risks we've already mentioned, excess weight is also associated with an increased risk of depression. Overweight- and obesity-related depression could be due to chemical imbalances within the body, but it could also be linked to the discrimination and low *self-esteem* that many people suffering from overweight and obesity experience.

People who are overweight or obese in childhood have a greatly increased chance of becoming overweight or obese adults. Today, overweight and obesity are occurring in greater rates at younger ages. Not surprisingly, as these conditions set in earlier, the health risks that come with excess weight also set in earlier. As Americans begin suffering with problems like high cholesterol and type 2 diabetes at an earlier age, life expectancy will also be reduced. Clearly, there are many reasons why people should strive to maintain a healthy weight throughout their lives, but what is a healthy weight, and how does a person know if he is overweight or obese?

> *"Individuals who are obese . . . have a 50 to 100 percent increased risk of premature death from all causes, compared to individuals with a healthy weight."* (from The United States Surgeon General's Web site)

Understanding Overweight and Obesity

Today, the majority of American adults and a large portion of America's young people are overweight, but many people have difficulty judging whether their weight is a healthy one or not. On the one hand, magazines, movies, television shows, and other media sources show us images of ridiculously thin people. These images are neither realistic nor healthy, and those who wish to obtain these pencil-thin bodies often have a skewed understanding of what a healthy body should look like. On the other hand, millions of Americans are overweight, and when seeing overweight bodies every day, we may begin to see these bodies as the norm. But being overweight is not healthy either, and when constantly faced with these two extremes—too thin and too heavy—a person can quickly lose sight of what a healthy body should look like. When discussing overweight and obesity, we must remember that the most important thing is not to achieve a specific *look*. The most important thing is to achieve *good health*.

The first thing to understand about weight is that every person's body is different. No one can say, "130 pounds is the optimal weight," or, "150

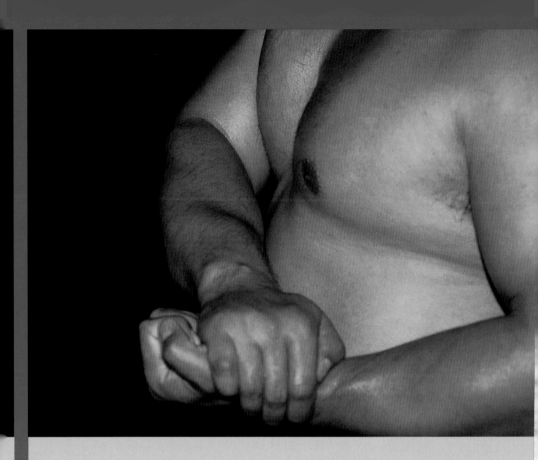

pounds is an unhealthy weight." The weight that is healthy for you depends on many factors, like your height, age, sex, fitness level, and *genetics*. In fact, weight alone isn't a very good measurement of whether or not you are a healthy body size. For example, if I told you that a person weighed 230 pounds, you might immediately assume the person I was discussing was overweight. But perhaps the person I was discussing was a six-foot-five-inch-tall male wrestler. In this case, our 230-pound person might not be overweight at all and might in fact be very athletic and healthy.

Since weight is not always a good determinant of body size or health, doctors rely on other tools to determine overweight and obesity. One tool doctors use to evaluate body size is body mass index (BMI). BMI is a mathematical formula that uses weight and height to determine whether someone's body is a healthy size. The formula is as follows:

[Weight in pounds ÷ (Height in inches x Height in inches)] x 703 = BMI

or

[Weight in kilograms ÷ (Height in centimeters x Height in centimeters)] x 10,000 = BMI

If a person's BMI formula yields a number below 18.5, a doctor would classify that person as being underweight (which can be a serious health threat of its own). A BMI that falls anywhere between 18.5 and 24.9 is considered a normal or healthy weight. If a person's BMI falls between 25.0 and 29.9, he would be considered overweight, and a person who has a BMI of 30.0 or above would be classified as obese. Here is an example for a person who weighs 132 pounds and is five feet, four inches (64 inches) tall:

[132 pounds ÷ (64 inches x 64 inches)] x 703 = 22.66 (a normal weight)

Since BMI takes a person's height into account, it is a better measure of healthy body size than weight alone, but it is still not always an accurate measure of health. For example, muscle tissue is much denser and heavier than fat tissue. Since BMI only measures height and weight, an extremely muscular and fit person could have the same BMI as an unfit person who has a large amount of fat. In fact, according to the BMI formula, our 230-pound wrestler would have a BMI of 27.3 and would therefore be considered overweight. His additional poundage, however, could be pure muscle. For this reason, the National Institutes of Health (NIH) suggests that BMI should be combined with other information, like waist circumference and other risk factors, for a more accurate evaluation of a person's overall health. According to the NIH, men whose waists measure over forty inches and women whose waists measure over thirty-five inches are at a greater risk for developing

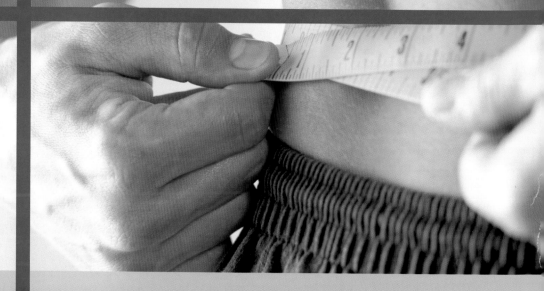

weight-related health problems. Additional risk factors include high blood pressure and elevated cholesterol, triglyceride, or blood-sugar levels; a family history of heart disease; physical inactivity; and smoking. A person who has a high BMI, a high waist circumference, and two or more risk factors is at high risk of developing weight-related health problems. A doctor would typically recommend that such a person lose weight.

BMI is not the only way to measure a person's body size and determine his risk for weight-related health problems. Another measure of overweight and obesity is body fat percentage—the amount of your body's tissue that is made of fat. To calculate a person's body fat percentage, a trained professional, like a doctor, nutritionist, or fitness expert, measures different areas of the person's body with special tools called calipers and a measuring tape. The calipers, which look like pinchers, gently pinch excess flesh, measuring the amount of excess flesh on key areas of the body. These measurements yield the person's body fat percentage. Body fat percentages can be excellent measures of overall health because they distinguish between lean tissue (your muscles, bones, organs, blood, and other body tissues) and fat tissue. For example, if you were a person who weighed 135 pounds and had a body fat percentage of 20 percent, that would mean your body contained twenty-seven pounds of fat and 108 pounds of lean tissue. Below are the ranges for body fat percentage and their corresponding health categories:

Essential Fat:	Women 10–12%, Men 2–4%
Athletes:	Women 14–20%, Men 6–13%
Fitness:	Women 21–24%, Men 14–17%
Acceptable:	Women 25–31%, Men 18–25%
Obese:	Women 32% +, Men 25% +

As you can see, neither BMI nor body fat percentage gives one number that is optimal for all people. Instead, these measurements yield a *range* of numbers that can be healthy or unhealthy. Perhaps most significantly, body fat percentage has different ranges for women and men. This is because women's and men's bodies function differently. Some fat is essential to all people's health, and women's bodies require a greater amount of fat to function properly. Men's bodies tend to be more muscular and need significantly less fat.

Knowing one's BMI or body fat percentage, however, is only part of the story. Knowing how our bodies get to be a healthy or unhealthy weight and how to correct overweight or obesity if they occur is much more important.

chapter 3

The Fitness Factor: The Foundation of Good Health

- Battle of the Pyramids

- Made to Move

- The Calorie Connection: Understanding Energy Intake

- The Fitness Factor: Understanding Energy Output

Battle of the Pyramids

If you are like most Americans, you are probably familiar with something called the Food Guide Pyramid. In 1992, the United States Department of Agriculture (USDA) created the Food Guide Pyramid as an easy-to-understand reference tool, and since then it has been promoted as the ultimate model for healthy eating. It appears on the back of cereal boxes, it is pictured on posters hung in doctors' offices, and it is taught in our schools. In 2005, the pyramid was replaced with MyPyramid.

Faculty members at the Harvard School of Public Health believe the USDA's new pyramid is still incorrect and misleading in the types and amounts of foods it recommended people eat for good health. For example, the USDA's pyramid makes no distinction between healthy carbohydrates

What you do is as important as what you eat.

(like whole grains) and unhealthy carbohydrates (like white bread and pasta) or between healthy fats (like olive and vegetable oils) and unhealthy fats (like those in butter and red meat). Furthermore, the Harvard study concluded that the USDA's pyramid overlooked a basic fact: even if a person ate the healthiest diet possible, if that person did not exercise he would still not be healthy. As a result of their findings, Harvard University created its own pyramid, and its foundation is not a food at all; it's physical activity. This is because the Harvard researchers recognized that in the quest for good health, what you do is as important as what you eat.

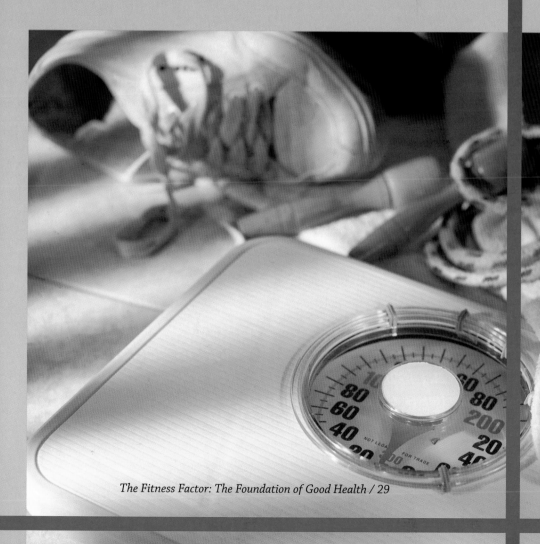

The Fitness Factor: The Foundation of Good Health / 29

Made to Move

The human body evolved to be active nearly every waking moment of every day. Early humans were probably about as fit and strong as today's marathon runners, but not because they trained, worked out, or spent hours on a treadmill. The effort it took simply to survive gave the average human more than enough exercise to make her as fit as today's most formidable athletes. Life was hard for early humans, and the mere task of finding food consumed most of their time and energy. In fact, early humans probably spent nearly every moment of every day searching, chasing after, and fighting for their food. Even as our societies became much more advanced, benefiting from things like agriculture and increased technologies, the daily tasks of living still required a constant output of energy. Plowing fields or hauling water from a well may be improvements on chasing down wild animals or hiking miles to a river, but they are still exhausting, backbreaking activities. Furthermore, additional tasks necessary for daily survival, like building and maintaining shelter, making clothing, caring for children, and protecting the community, also required great physical labor.

All around the world, people still labor nearly every moment of the day to attain their food, water, clothing, shelter, and other life necessities. In areas where lifestyles are still lived much as they were centuries ago, obesity and its related health risks are virtually nonexistent. This is in stark contrast

The majority of Americans suffer from an imbalance in this formula: they use less energy than they take in.

with the United States and other *industrialized* countries where *sedentary* lifestyles are perhaps the number-one contributor to rising obesity rates. Weight gain or loss depends on a relatively simple formula. To maintain your current weight, your energy intake must equal your energy output. The majority of Americans suffer from an imbalance in this formula: they use less energy than they take in.

The Calorie Connection: Understanding Energy Intake

With every second that passes, your body uses energy. You could compare your body to a car. A car needs energy to make it run. To get that energy, the car needs an energy-rich raw material. Most of our cars run on gasoline, a fuel that contains lots of potential energy. The gasoline gets pumped through the car's engine and burned. The process of changing a raw material into energy is quite complicated, but ultimately the potential energy in the gasoline gets converted to kinetic energy (the energy of motion), and the car moves. If the fuel runs out, the car stops moving. Similarly, your body takes in raw mate-

rials in the form of food and metabolizes those materials to supply the energy your body needs to function.

We measure the amount of energy in food with a unit called a Calorie. A Calorie is a thermal unit of energy; it is an amount of heat. Calorie with a capital "C" stands for large calorie or kilogram calorie. This is the type of Calorie used to measure energy in food. One Calorie is equal to the amount of energy it would take to heat one kilogram of water (approximately one liter or four and a quarter cups) one degree Celsius. There is also a measurement known as a *small calorie*, or calorie with a lowercase "c." This type of calorie is used in chemistry, physics, and other disciplines that need to measure accurately tiny amounts of heat. A small calorie is the amount of heat it takes to heat one gram of water (one milliliter or about twenty drops from an eyedropper) one degree Celsius. There are one thousand small calories in a single food Calorie. That's a lot of energy!

You require energy for absolutely everything you do. Every time your heart beats, your lungs take in air, your stomach digests, your brain thinks, or your muscles move, you are burning Calories. The more your body is doing, the more Calories you will burn. You even burn Calories while you are sleeping! When you are active and need lots of energy, your body immediately burns the Calories you consume. For example, if you eat breakfast then head outside to play a game or head off to school to learn, your body immediately begins burning the fuel you've taken in. If you do not need the Calories you are taking in, however, your body will store that extra energy as fat. This might happen when, for example, you plop down in front of the TV with a snack and spend the next three hours vegging out. Storing some of your Calories as fat, however, is not always bad. A couple days later you might burn more Calories than you take in. Then your body dips into its fat reserves to get the extra energy you need.

Most people do not count exactly how many Calories they take in and burn every day. This involves some very complicated mathematics and can require the help of health professionals. It is, however, quite easy to tell if

Most people think they need 2,000 Calories each day. This is a misconception. If you look at the average nutrition label on a box of food, you will probably see the phrase "Based on a 2,000 Calorie diet." A 2,000 Calorie diet, however, is just a convenient average. In reality, different people need different amounts of Calories. For example, teenagers, males, people with large bodies, and very active people usually require more Calories than older people, females, people with small bodies, or people who are inactive. According to the USDA, teenage girls and active women require approximately 2,200 Calories each day, while teenage boys and active men require approximately 2,800 Calories each day.

you are burning more or fewer Calories than you are taking in. If you are taking in more Calories than you are burning, you will gain weight. If you are taking in fewer Calories than you are burning, you will lose weight. If your weight stays stable over time, you are burning the same amount of Calories as you take in.

It is important to remember that weight gain or loss only tells you if you are burning the energy you take in; it does not tell you how many Calories you need. For example, perhaps you are using the same number of Calories you take in every day and are therefore neither gaining nor losing weight. You could still, however, be getting too few Calories. If so, you would feel tired, run-down, and unable to perform numerous physical activities. If you ate more Calories, you would have more energy, could be more active, and still burn all the Calories you take in. Many people, however, take in more

Calories each day than they burn and therefore gain excess weight. When people find themselves gaining weight, the first word to come to their lips is often *diet*. For many Americans today, however, the most helpful word would be *exercise*.

On the surface, it may seem that cutting back on Calories is the logical way to deal with weight gain. After all, fewer Calories taken in means fewer Calories to store as fat. Sometimes a change in diet is necessary and important to losing weight and improving health, but for most people changing diet alone is not the best way to deal with excess weight. After all, Calories are essential to your health, and without enough you won't have the energy you need to function. Furthermore, food doesn't just provide you with the Calories you need for energy. It also provides you with all the nutrients necessary to build and support your body's tissues and functions. Good health requires a combination of a healthy diet and physical activity, and for many people with excess weight, increasing activity may be the answer to achieving good health. When a person is having trouble finding the right balance between caloric intake and energy expenditure, seeking advice from a health professional such as a doctor, nurse, nutritionist, or fitness instructor is a good idea.

Good health requires a combination of a healthy diet and physical activity, and for many people with excess weight, increasing activity may be the answer to achieving good health.

The Fitness Factor: Understanding Energy Output

As we discussed in chapter 1, overweight and obesity are rising at epidemic rates. Thus the health risks associated with these conditions are also on the rise. These health risks, however, are not simply caused by carrying extra pounds. They are also caused by lack of exercise. Daily exercise is essential to keeping your bones and muscles strong and every part of your body in working order. When you don't get daily exercise, every muscle— from your leg muscles to your heart—gets weaker. Your bones lose strength. Body systems, like your respiratory, digestive, and immune systems, don't function as well. Joints lose flexibility, and your whole body slows down.

Think again about a car. What would happen to your car if you parked it in a garage and didn't drive it for months? The next time you needed to drive your car, would it start? Maybe . . . but maybe not. Like your body, a car is designed to be in motion. A car has many systems that must work together to make it run. When a car is being driven, many things are happening that are necessary for maintaining the car's life and parts. For example, the

To be fit and healthy, a person needs to spend a significant portion of every day engaged in physical activity.

battery is getting charged, fuel is being burned, and parts are being lubricated with oil. If left to sit for a long period of time without use, parts and systems within the car can begin to fail. Like a car, your body and its systems need constant exercise, or else there's no guarantee things will be in working order when you need them. Additionally, exercise plays an essential role in people's moods, self-esteem, and ability to handle stress.

Having a fit and healthy body is important to maintaining a healthy weight. The first reason for this is obvious: When your body is working hard, it requires lots of energy and will therefore burn lots of Calories. The second reason, however, may surprise you. Did you know that even when at rest a healthy body burns more Calories than an unhealthy body burns? Even when you are not doing anything on the outside, a lot of processes that require energy are taking place inside your body. For example, your body must constantly maintain a temperature of approximately 98.6 degrees Fahrenheit (37 degrees Celsius). To do this requires energy. Even when at rest, lean tissue (your muscles, bones, organs, blood, etc.) requires much more energy than fat tissue requires. The rate at which your body uses energy is called your metabolism rate, and a person with a high percentage of lean tissue and a low percentage of body fat will have a higher metabolism rate than a person with a low percentage of lean tissue and high percentage of body fat.

So what does a person need to do to get fit and healthy? Thousands of books, magazine articles, doctors' pamphlets, and television shows have been devoted to this topic, but in the end, the answer is relatively simple: To be fit and healthy, a person needs to spend a significant portion of every day engaged in physical activity. For young people, this means spending a *minimum* of one hour each day engaged in moderate to vigorous activity. This doesn't necessarily mean that you have to be running for an hour, but your body does have to be in motion. If you walk or ride a bike to school, play sports on a regular basis, or even spend significant time doing things like vacuuming the house or mowing the lawn with a push mower, you are already engaging in physical activity. If your daily physical activity, however, doesn't add up to at least an hour, you need to add exercise to your lifestyle.

Though the most important thing might be to get your body in motion, any motion, not all exercise is the same. If you are to be truly fit and healthy, you need to get different types of exercise that will benefit your whole body.

chapter 4

Getting Started: Adding Exercise to Your Life

- Not All Exercise Is the Same

- Getting Started

- Break Through Your Barriers

Not All Exercise Is the Same

Although the most important thing is to get your body moving, to be as healthy as you can be, you need certain types of exercise. Broadly speaking, there are two categories of exercise. The first category, aerobic exercise, increases your heart and breathing rates and strengthens your *cardiovascular* and *respiratory* systems. Running, playing basketball, cycling, and cross-country skiing are all examples of aerobic activities. Aerobic activities need to be sustained for at least twenty minutes, however, before they begin strengthening your heart and lungs and burning fat.

Not only does aerobic exercise need to be sustained at least twenty minutes to be beneficial, it also needs to be sustained at an elevated heart rate. To achieve cardiovascular and respiratory benefits, most young people should strive to maintain a heart rate of 140 to 170 beats per minute during aerobic activity. To check your heart rate, press your index and middle fingers lightly on the inside of your wrist or on your neck just below and inside of your jawbone. Count the number of times you feel your pulse in a minute, or count for six seconds and multiply that number by ten. If you're not achieving a heart rate of 140 beats per minute, increase your activity level. If your heart is racing above 170, decrease your activity to a more comfortable rate.

The second type of exercise, anaerobic exercise, strengthens your musculoskeletal system but does not necessarily benefit your heart and lungs. Weight lifting, push-ups, leg lifts, and abdominal crunches are all examples of anaerobic exercise. While aerobic exercise needs to be sustained to increase heart strength, anaerobic exercise usually involves short bursts of intense resistance-based activity.

A recent study by a team of Yale University researchers found that some weight lifters may be at risk of rupturing the aorta (the main artery coming from the heart) during workouts. The muscles in your body contract when you lift a weight causing a spike in your blood pressure. The heavier the weight, the stronger the muscular contraction is, and the stronger the contraction, the larger the spike is. In a number of cases, this blood-pressure spike has caused the lifter's aorta to tear open. The team of researchers believes that people who already have weak arteries due to genetics or other factors are at the greatest risk for this type of injury. Further research is under way.

Anaerobic activity is very important for your body's overall health and strength, but teens in particular should be careful about the type and amount of anaerobic activity they choose. Many people enjoy weight lifting as a way of increasing strength, but according to some studies, lifting heavy weights before a person is fully grown can actually damage the musculoskeletal system and stunt development. Strength training using moderate amounts of weight is generally not harmful. Power lifting and bodybuilding, however, can be dangerous and should only be engaged in by people who are completely done growing. For most people, growth stops between ages sixteen and eighteen, but it can end even later in males. Serious weight lifting is best left until adolescent development has fully run its course.

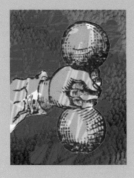

Getting Started

Many people are under the mistaken impression that aerobic exercise is the most important type of exercise and that anaerobic exercise is just for people who want big muscles. This is not true at all. Having a mixture of aerobic and anaerobic activities in your daily life is essential to developing overall fitness and good health. It is true that aerobic exercise benefits your heart and lungs and, if

> *The more lean tissue you have, the higher your metabolism will be and the more Calories you will burn, even when at rest.*

sustained long enough, burns body fat. Strength training in the form of anaerobic exercise, however, also bestows huge benefits. Remember our discussion of body fat percentage in chapter 1? There we said that lean tissue (your muscles, bones, organs, etc.) is denser and heavier than fat tissue. We also said that lean tissue takes more energy to maintain than fat tissue requires. That means the more lean tissue you have, the higher your metabolism will be and the more Calories you will burn, even when at rest. Luckily, many activities offer a combination of aerobic and anaerobic benefits. Swimming, for example, is aerobic because it increases your heart and breathing rates. However, the water also provides resistance to all of your muscles, so swimming has anaerobic benefits as well.

So how much of each type of exercise do you need? We've already stated you need at least one hour of physical activity (like walking or riding a bike to school, participating in gym class, playing basketball or other games with friends, gardening, and even cleaning) each day, but if this activity doesn't increase your heart rate and strengthen your muscles, you will need to add aerobic and anaerobic activities to your life. Doctors recommend a minimum of twenty minutes of moderately vigorous aerobic activity at least three times a week as either a part of or in addition to your daily hour of activity. But remember, things like television, video games, computers, and other sedentary pastimes have drastically reduced the amount of time the average person spends moving. Moving, plain and simple, is vital to good health, and a planned aerobic exercise regime should be in addition to your other daily

movement and activity. If you spend most of every day engaged in sedentary activities, then twenty minutes of exercise three times a week is not going to be enough to make you healthy. You don't need to "work out" seven days a week, but you *must* be active every single day.

Just like aerobic activity, anaerobic activity also needs to be a regular part of your routine. Muscle is a body tissue in which the saying "use it or lose it"

If you are not engaging your muscles every day, they quickly deteriorate and get converted to fat for storage.

really applies. If you are not engaging your muscles every day, they quickly deteriorate and get converted to fat for storage. Daily strength-building activities are also vital to developing and maintaining strong bones. You probably don't have time, however, to do strength-building exercises for every part of your body every day. Alternating between your upper and lower body is a good approach to daily anaerobic exercise. For example, if you started every Monday, Wednesday, and Friday morning with some leg lifts and stomach crunches, and began every Sunday, Tuesday, and Thursday (let's say you take off Saturday mornings) with some push-ups, you'd already be well on your way to strengthening most of your muscles each day. Alternating muscle groups also reduces your chance of injury. Many people, however, feel intimidated by the thought of lifting weights or doing push-ups. Luckily, there are many other ways to engage in anaerobic exercise. Activities like yoga and dance, for example, are great ways to strengthen your muscles and bones. They are also fun, and exercising in a class or group can help to get you motivated.

Break Through Your Barriers

Every human being, whether or not she is a healthy weight, needs daily exercise. Even though we know exercise is important, however, many of us still don't get the exercise we need. Lack of time isn't the only thing holding us back. There are other barriers to beginning an exercise routine. Some of the most common ones are mental: self-consciousness, low self-esteem, and embarrassment. Perhaps you feel you'd "rather die" than be seen in a swimsuit. Maybe you think you're too uncoordinated to play a group sport or be seen in an aerobics class. Or maybe you just have a general fear of failure that keeps you from getting started in the first place.

All of these are common concerns, but they are no excuse for jeopardizing your health! The first thing to remember is that as common as these fears are, they are usually unfounded. If you are doing laps in a pool, exercising at a gym, or playing a sport, chances are the people around you are way too busy counting their own laps, focusing on their workouts, or concentrating on the game to care what you look like in a swimsuit or how your coordination is. Furthermore, many of those people probably suffer from similar fears, but are you looking for their faults and judging their performance? Hopefully not—you (like everyone else) have more important things to worry about.

If you still find fear and self-consciousness getting in your way, however, remember there are lots of ways to exercise in private or in a small group. Brisk walking is something you can do by yourself or with friends without feeling self-conscious. As your fitness level increases, you can experiment with increasing your walk to a jog or even a run. Home exercise equipment and activities like jumping rope and jumping jacks are also ways to exercise in private. For most people, exercising is a great way to realize their bodies' abilities and potential. As your fitness level improves, your self-esteem and confidence will also get a boost, and before long you may be ready to tackle bigger challenges or join group activities.

Another important thing to remember is that you don't have to start out big. If you have not been exercising regularly, do not start your first day by trying to run a marathon or break world records. Instead, make a steady effort to build up your strength and stamina over time. Even simple physical activities expend energy and are important steps on the road to fitness.

Even if you are determined to become healthy, however, there are still a lot of things that may be standing in your way. Unfortunately, lack of exercise and unhealthy lifestyles are no longer individual problems; they are national problems. The American way of life has changed drastically in the last one hundred years, and many of the changes it has undergone contribute to the obesity epidemic.

Chapter 5

What You Are Up Against: America's Unhealthy Lifestyle

- Fast Food and Growing Portion Sizes

- Living the Sedentary Lifestyle

- Advertising

- Confused Priorities: A Tragedy in Our Schools

Lots of people like to claim that individuals must take personal responsibility for how much they eat and exercise, and if a person becomes overweight, it is his or her own fault. This may sound reasonable at first, but taking personal responsibility can be much more difficult than it seems. That's because in America today there are all kinds of factors influencing the way you live your life, including the choices you make about food and activity. Unfortunately, you are up against some *formidable* opponents in your quest to eat right and exercise more. Let's take a closer look at just a few of the factors contributing to America's obesity crisis: fast food and growing portion sizes, sedentary lifestyles, advertising, and changes in our schools.

Fast Food and Growing Portion Sizes

Every day, thousands of companies vie for a piece of you—or rather, a piece of your wallet. Not only will much of what they sell *not* help you be healthier, much of it will make you *unhealthier*. Today, many American companies are contributing to the obesity crisis, and at the front lines of these corporate warriors are fast-food companies.

Fast food is all around you. Fast-food restaurants seem to grace every corner of every town, their golden arches, neon lights, and pictures of juicy burgers and crisp fries beckoning to you and your stomach. Fast food, however, isn't just in restaurants anymore. It's also all over grocery store shelves and packing vending machines in all of your favorite hangouts. Today's

Americans have busy lives, and thousands of prepared, prepackaged products promise to ease the burden of dinnertime.

Many a busy parent or study-strained student will tell you that it's great to be able to grab dinner at a drive-through or throw a frozen meal in the oven and have it ready twenty minutes later. These conveniences are certainly helpful when it comes to saving time. But when it comes to our health, there's a big problem. The vast majority of fast food is extremely unhealthy. Most of it is high in fat, Calories, and salt or sugar, and low in essential nutrients and fiber. If you eat fast food on a regular basis, whether it comes from a restaurant, grocery store, or vending machine, you may be well on your way to packing on extra pounds or depriving yourself of the nutrients necessary for good health.

Of course some fast foods are healthier than others, and today thousands of products from low-fat meals to vegetarian *entrees* are cropping up to

> Today the portion sizes of some foods (especially fast foods) are many times what they were just twenty or even ten years ago.

appeal to the health-conscious consumer. Are these fast foods also unhealthy? Not necessarily, but be careful. Look at ingredients and nutrition labels so you know what's really in that food; some companies like to get on the healthy bandwagon without really providing truly healthy food. Also keep in mind that most of these prepackaged meals are extremely expensive. You could make the same thing yourself for a lot less money, and prepackaged meals can rarely provide the nutrients that come from foods made with fresh produce and whole grains like brown rice, whole oats, whole wheat, and barley.

Fast foods that are high in fat, Calories, and salt aren't the only problem you may be facing at mealtimes. Another disturbing trend is the increase in portion sizes. If you have ever traveled outside of the United States, you may have noticed an interesting phenomenon. Perhaps you went into a coffee shop or a restaurant and ordered a beverage. Maybe you ordered a small because that is what you normally order at home in the United States. When you got your small drink, you may have blinked twice. It was really, really small! Or perhaps you ordered a large because that is what you normally order at home. If so, then you definitely blinked twice, and perhaps you said, "Excuse me. I ordered a large." If so, your American-ness was suddenly on display for everyone to see.

Most Americans never travel outside of America, so we don't necessarily realize that other people around the world don't eat or live as we do. In fact,

America is quite famous around the world for its "bigness." "In America," people say, "everything is big—big country, big houses, big cars, big money, big food, big drinks, and big people." On the one hand, this is a *stereotype*, and stereotypes are never all true. On the other hand, stereotypes sometimes arise from actual circumstances, and in the case of American eating habits, the stereotypes are largely right.

Today the portion sizes of some foods (especially fast foods) are many times what they were just twenty or even ten years ago. In some cases they have grown grossly out of proportion with the human body. A study published by the *Journal of the American Medical Association* found that between the years 1971 and 1999, portion sizes for certain foods increased dramatically. Of the foods studied—hamburgers, Mexican food, soft drinks, snacks, and pizza—all but pizza increased. Hamburgers became, on average, more than a fifth larger. A plate of Mexican food was more than one-quarter larger. Soft drinks had expanded by more than half their previous size, and salty snacks like potato chips, pretzels, and crackers had grown by 60 percent. The most striking increases occurred in fast-food restaurants, but perhaps most disturbingly, these portion increases occurred in the American home as well. Whether eating out or eating in, Americans are eating more than ever before, and you can bet that those extra Calories are a factor in the rising obesity crisis.

Recently, researchers at Penn State University's College of Health and Human Development wanted to see if people's hunger mechanisms would stand up to increased portion sizes. In their study, they gave volunteers different size portions of macaroni and cheese and told them to eat until they were full. The results astounded the researchers. When the volunteers were given smaller portions, they stopped eating sooner, even if they didn't clean their plates. When given a larger portion, the volunteers ate an average of 30 percent more (again even if they didn't clean their plates) and did not report feeling fuller. The volunteers did not realize they had eaten more at the large-portion sittings, and most didn't even notice the portion size had increased.

When McDonald's, perhaps the most famous of the fast-food restaurants, opened its doors for the first time, it didn't even have medium and large options. Fries were fries, and they came in what today would look like a very small package. Today, however, slogans like "Get more for your money!" and "Bigger is better!" are fast-food *mantras*. Practically every fast-food restaurant has its own version of the "value meal." Wendy's has Biggie® drinks, Biggie® fries, and if those aren't big enough, a Great Biggie® size. Burger King has King drinks and King fries, and until recently McDonald's had the famous Supersize®. In some restaurants, what was once a regular-size fries or drink is now the "kiddie size," and what used to be a large is now a small!

Living the Sedentary Lifestyle

An increasing dependence on fast food and growing portion sizes would be disturbing just on their own, but combined with another factor—decreasing activity—they are especially alarming. We Americans are not only eating more than ever before, we're also less active than we've ever been. As we discussed in chapter 3, the human body did not evolve to sit in a car, behind a desk, in front of a computer, or before a television. It evolved to be in motion. Yet for many of us, riding in cars and sitting at desks are exactly the types of activities that take up the majority of our time.

Human society certainly hasn't always been as American society is today. For about 99 percent of human history (and still for most humans in the world) people never had to think about exercising because their whole lives involved exercise. *Foraging* and hunting took huge amounts of energy. Farming is also exhausting, backbreaking, Calorie-burning work. Even with the rise of the Industrial Age, when many people in the *Western* world left farming to make money in mines, factories, and industry-driven trades, most of the work was still just as physical and exhausting. It's really only

For about 99 percent of human history (and still for most humans in the world) people never had to think about exercising because their whole lives involved exercise.

within the last fifty to sixty years that American lifestyles changed so dramatically. So what happened? How did our bodies go from being Calorie-burning machines to Calorie-storage systems?

Numerous factors have *coalesced* to produce our inactive lifestyle. Perhaps one of the most important was the invention of the car, a form of transportation that requires almost no physical exertion from us to get us where we're going. Before the invention of the car, many people lived in urban areas (except of course for farmers who lived in rural areas) where they were close to work and services. With the age of the automobile, however, people no longer needed to live within easy walking and cycling distances—they could get in a car and drive, and suburbs were born. Millions of people left urban areas for what would become the more-desirable suburbs. A flight to the suburbs made people dependent on cars to get to work, school, grocery stores, friends' houses, and other destinations. Today, Americans spend more hours in the car than ever before, and recent studies have shown that the longer a person spends in the car each day, the more likely he is to develop weight-related disorders.

At the same time that cars and suburban living have reduced the physical exertion it takes to get to and from work, a switch to a *service-based economy* has put more of us in offices and sedentary jobs. With much of our time spent at work (or at school), the only time left for exercise is leisure time. But technologies like televisions and computers have made much of our leisure time sedentary as well. Just because much of our work is no longer physical, however, doesn't mean it's not exhausting, and after a long day at school or work, most of us find it easier to plop down in front of the television than to go exercise.

The movement toward a sedentary lifestyle is definitely contributing to the increase in obesity. Remember our discussion of Calories? There we said that different people need different amounts of Calories based on things like age, sex, size, and activity level.

Well, think about this: The average active woman needs about 2,200 Calories each day, and the average active man needs 2,800 Calories each day. In a perfect world, we would all be active. But our world is not perfect; not only are we all not active, most of us are inactive. If you are an inactive woman, you will probably only need 1,500 to 1,800 Calories each day, while an inactive man will likely only need 2,000 to 2,200. That's a big difference from active people. When sedentary lifestyles, which require relatively few Calories to maintain, combine with Calorie-rich fast foods and growing portion sizes, you have a sure recipe for overweight and obesity.

Advertising

Even with a reliance on cars, sedentary pastimes, and an unhealthy diet, aren't most people still responsible for the lifestyle choices that they make? Can't you just choose to exercise more and eat healthier? Yes and no. America is a capitalist country—it relies on private business to support the economy. These businesses sell products and services, and as we've just seen, much of what they sell (like fast and prepackaged foods, cars, televisions, and computers) contributes to rising obesity rates. A business's goal is to make money—as much money as possible—so these businesses can't just encourage you to give up their products in the interest of your health. If they did, and if you listened, they couldn't make any money! They want you to buy their products and buy them often. To encourage you to do this, they use a very powerful tool: advertising. Every year companies spend billions and billions of dollars on advertising to "help" you make choices about what you will eat, what you will buy, and how you will spend your time.

Over the years, advertising has changed in an important way. It used to be almost solely directed at adults. The reason was quite logical. Adults have the jobs, and adults have the money, so messages about where to spend that

money should be aimed at those adults. But there's also a problem in advertising to adults—they have years of experience and well-developed tastes that make a lot of advertising easy to resist. But some companies learned an important advertising lesson early on. Children are easier to persuade than adults, and children usually have more influence with their parents than companies have. If a company could get *children* to want a product, those children would go to their parents, beg and plead, and often be successful in getting what

Every year companies spend billions and billions of dollars on advertising to "help" you make choices about what you will eat, what you will buy, and how you will spend your time.

According to Marion Nestle of New York University's Department of Nutrition and Food Studies, about half of all advertisements directed toward children are for food. Ms. Nestle estimates that the food and drink industries spend $13 billion each year advertising to kids.

they wanted. When an advertisement aimed at an adult was successful, it might bring in one customer. When an advertisement aimed at a child was successful, it often brought in three or more customers (the child and the child's parents and siblings). Today, all kinds of manufacturers, from those who make food, to video games, to cars, realize that the best way to get into Mom's or Dad's pocket is through the child. Kids mean big money.

Companies that advertised to children learned another important lesson: a child converted will be a customer for life. Companies believed that if they could get a child to become loyal to their brand and products early on, that child would remain loyal for the rest of his life. For example, a child who started eating McDonald's before he tasted Burger King, the theory went, would continue eating McDonald's. A child who started drinking Coke before she tasted Pepsi would always prefer Coke. A person who had pleasant memories of slurping milk shakes as a child would slurp milk shakes as an adult. The companies were right. Brand loyalty, a person's commitment to a specific brand, often has less to do with the actual quality of the product than with how early and successfully the brand can be *ingratiated* into the person's consciousness.

Today, all kinds of people are employed in the business of marketing to children, and they use numerous tools to figure out how. Psychiatrists give analysis of children's dreams. Researchers explore the affects of bright colors on the child brain. Artists and designers develop eye-catching logos and child-friendly characters. One can say that every individual is responsible for

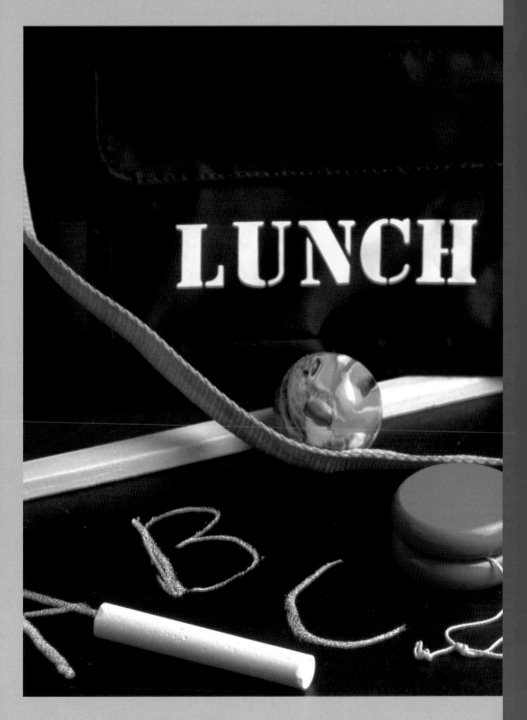

> "The challenge of the campaign is to make customers believe that McDonald's is their 'Trusted Friend.'"
> —*Ray Bergold, McDonald's marketing executive*

her own lifestyle choices, but young children are largely powerless against this advertising onslaught. Studies have shown that young children can't distinguish between regular television entertainment and commercials. They don't know that they are being seduced by advertising and that their minds, emotions, and desires are being carefully manipulated by people with huge amounts of money, research, and expertise. They also don't yet have the skills to determine if advertising claims are trustworthy or not. If you tell a young child that a candy bar will make her strong, for example, she will believe you.

Children are defenseless against advertising, and many of the businesses that sell unhealthy products know it. According to James McNeal, author of *Kids as Customers* and *The Kids' Market: Myths and Realities*, companies begin influencing children when they are as young as two years old. By the time they are three, many children can recognize brand logos. Furthermore, exhausted parents often feel defenseless against their children's constant nagging. Businesses know this too and put lots of research money into finding the best way to *exploit* what they call the "nag factor."

Young children, however, aren't the only ones being targeted by advertising. In the last twenty years, teens have emerged as a huge market force. Besides money received as allowances or gifts, many teens work. Teens today have more *disposable income* than they have ever had before. Each year, teens spend more than $150 billion from their own pockets. That's a huge amount of money, and companies selling unhealthy foods and sedentary entertainment want to get their share. To make sure they are getting as much of young people's money as possible, corporations have embarked on a huge and disturbing trend. They've moved into your schools.

Confused Priorities: A Tragedy in Our Schools

Today, the obesity crisis is brewing in the halls of our educational institutions, and two major changes are contributing to this situation: an increasing corporate presence within schools and a decrease in physical education and activities.

Many American schools have faced serious financial difficulties in recent decades. Cuts in government spending, opposition to tax increases, and increasing student enrollments have left some schools gasping for funds. When corporations, especially food and soft drink manufacturers, began offering thousands of dollars for the privilege of getting their products and advertisements into schools, many districts rushed to sign up. Advertising on television and in print was good, but young people still had the power to turn off the TV or put down the magazine. Furthermore, if they're not on summer vacation, young people are spending most of each day at school where they can't watch television or read magazines. If food and beverage companies could get into the schools, they could not only reach children and teens during this otherwise *inaccessible* part of the day, they could have them as a captive audience as well. After all, you can't just walk out of a school because you don't want to see an advertisement.

Food and beverage companies not only have their vending machines in the hallways, advertisements on the walls, billboards on school buses, and logos plastered at sports events. They have also taken over many school lunch programs. America's government-sponsored school lunch program was never completely healthy to begin with, but today it has definitely taken a turn for the worse. For many schools, gone are the days of a sloppy joe, mashed potatoes, an apple, and a carton of milk. Now many children and teens go to the school cafeteria to grab pizza, cheeseburgers, chips, Coke,

Pepsi, and fries. Depending on their contracts, schools may even get a percentage of the fast-food or beverage sales. Worse yet, some schools have contracts that *stipulate* minimum sales *quotas*; if those quotas aren't met, the school can lose some of the promised revenues. This has led to some schools allowing soft drinks and snacks to be purchased in the hallways and consumed in the classrooms. The need for money to support their programs has turned some schools into *accomplices* of the very industries that contribute to rising obesity rates. Some schools now work with these industries to encourage fast-food consumption and maximize sales.

The presence of fast foods in schools *undermines* parents' ability to make healthy food choices for their children. More than that, it gives fast-food and beverage companies easy access to young people whose eating habits and lifestyles are still developing. Studies show that the habits we form when we are young usually stay with us for life and are the most difficult to break. A person who starts smoking at a young age will fight a difficult battle if she wants to quit and may very well end up smoking for life. Similarly, a person who starts eating fast food and drinking sugary soft drinks on a regular basis early on will carry those eating habits into adulthood and may end up fighting a lifelong battle against obesity.

At the same time that schools are opening their doors to businesses (like the fast-food and beverage industries) hawking unhealthy lifestyles, schools are being forced to eliminate healthy programs like recess and physical education. Again, budget cuts and other financial difficulties are partly to blame. When a school needs to cut back on expenses, it can't just cut the math program or the English program. Physical education and recess are usually lower priorities. Falling test scores in many schools around the nation also have administrators looking for ways to increase classroom and study time. Again, gym classes and recess are the first to go. But even if cutting physical activity from students' lives increased test scores (which new studies suggest is not the case), what good will this higher achievement level be if all our children are unhealthy? A healthy body is an integral part of a healthy, functioning mind, and when it comes to educating young people, we must be careful

WHEN LIGHT APPEARS IN PUSH BUTTON MAKE ANOTHER SELECTION

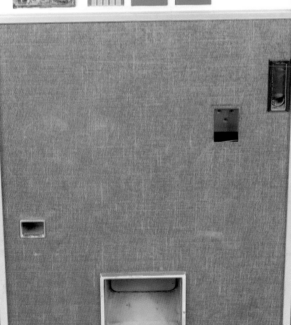

> *A person who starts eating fast food and drinking sugary soft drinks on a regular basis early on will carry those eating habits into adulthood and may end up fighting a lifelong battle against obesity.*

not to get our priorities confused. In some schools, young people now have greater access to unhealthy foods than they have to exercise—a tragedy that is contributing to the overweight and obesity crisis.

By now you should have a better understanding of the health risks of overweight and obesity, the importance of exercise, and some of the things you are up against in your quest to be healthy. But in case you think you must now become a fitness nut, here's something else for you to consider. Remember in chapter 1 we said that young people in America today faced a paradox? There we said that America is not only the heaviest nation on the earth, it's also the most image conscious. As you begin to think about exercise's role in your life, it's good to question this preoccupation with image that many of us have. Being too concerned with image can lead to problems of its own, and embarking on a fitness program in search of an unattainable ideal can have serious health risks.

Chapter 6

The Risks of Becoming Fitness Obsessed

- Supplement and Steroid Use

- Body Dysmorphic Disorder

- Anorexia Nervosa

- Bulimia Nervosa

Now that you have a better understanding of the risks of overweight and obesity and the benefits of exercise, it's time to ask new questions: Is it possible to exercise too much? Can a person be too fit? Can one become too focused on eating healthfully and exercising daily?

Surprising as it may sound, the answer is yes. Being healthy should be one of your most important goals, but it should not be an obsession. Furthermore, being healthy isn't just physical; it's also mental and emotional. So if you're a person who loves sleeping in late, spending a whole day lounging around, or snacking on some buttery popcorn while watching a movie, you shouldn't feel like you can never do these things.

If you want to be healthy, these activities cannot *be* your lifestyle. They

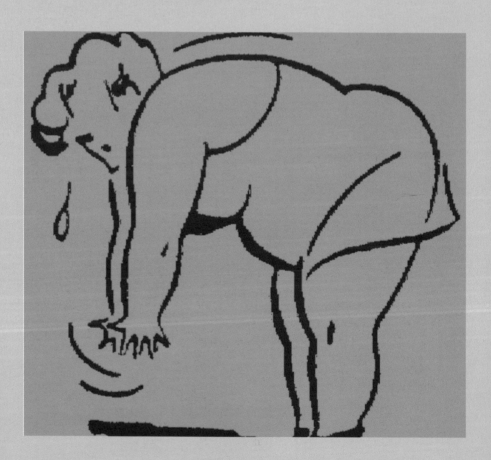

can, however, be enjoyed occasionally and can boost your mental and emotional health without jeopardizing your physical health. If you feel you can never take a day off from exercising or can never eat something you enjoy without feeling extreme guilt, you may be in danger of developing a fitness obsession.

Becoming obsessed with physical fitness can carry health risks of its own. For example, pushing your body too far too fast is a sure way to bring on injury. If you have to spend months not exercising while recovering from a serious injury, you will likely find your fitness level even lower (and your weight higher) than before you began exercising in the first place.

Besides injury, certain disorders and risky behaviors can also be associated with a health and fitness obsession. These risks may be higher if your fitness goals are image oriented rather than truly health oriented. One common and extremely risky behavior associated with image-oriented fitness obsession is the use of nutritional supplements and steroids.

Supplement and Steroid Use

Today many young people, especially young men, have become obsessed with having the perfectly cut, athletic bodies they see in magazines and on television. Spurred by an obsession with making their bodies big, some young men turn not just to behaviors like bodybuilding and nutritional supplements (which can also carry health risks), but also to using controlled substances known as anabolic steroids. Once seen almost exclusively in competitive male athletes, anabolic steroid use is on the rise among men who may not be athletes but want buff, athletic bodies. Steroid use has also become increasingly common among female athletes.

Anabolic steroids are synthetic chemicals that, when put in the body, act similarly to male sex hormones like testosterone. The major effect that anabolic steroids can produce is growth of the muscle tissues. The only way to legally obtain steroids is through a prescription, but a huge illegal drug trade has grown out of selling steroids to athletes and others who wish to grow bigger, stronger muscles.

Using anabolic steroids can have unpleasant side effects. The most common of these is an increase in male characteristics like body hair and a deepening voice. These particular side effects may be difficult to detect in men,

but they are usually quite noticeable in women who abuse steroids. Other side effects, such as breast growth and shrinking testicles, are common in men. Male-pattern baldness, acne, aggressive behavior, and rage are also common side effects that occur in both men and women. Life-threatening side effects may include heart attack and liver cancer. Most effects of steroid use reverse after one ceases taking the substances, but some side effects, like baldness, can be irreversible. It is also unclear what the long-term side effects of prolonged steroid use might be. Typically, your body produces the proper amount of hormones it needs and regulates its production depending on how many hormones are active in the body. Taking steroids severely disrupts your body's natural production of hormones by flooding your body with excessive amounts of the chemicals. Your endocrine system, the body system involved in the manufacture of hormones, then ceases its own natural production. Studies have not yet determined what the long-term effects of such system shutdowns will be.

Steroid use was once limited to the medical field where steroids can treat some forms of illness. Illegal use and abuse of steroids then spread to professional athletes who realized they could enhance strength and performance using these drugs. However, over the past three decades steroid use has been steadily rising in the larger population, and it is no longer limited to the community of professional athletes. Steroid abuse now *permeates* all levels of the population. Using steroids as part of a training program became disturbingly common among high school and college athletes in the 1980s. Throughout the 1990s, the growth rate of steroid use in high schools leveled off, and is currently holding relatively constant. One reason given for the halt in growth rates is education programs that have taught young people about the dangers of steroids. Another reason, however, may be that young people are simply switching from illegal steroids to legal supplements like creatine. Many young people think that, because nutritional supplements like creatine are legal and widely available, they must be safe. This is not necessarily true. Like steroids, the long-term effects of supplement use are not

During the 1990s, steroid use among teenage boys leveled off and was even reduced in some places. However, steroid use among teenage girls appears to have doubled.

yet known. Furthermore, many nutritional supplements are extremely high in protein. Although some protein is necessary for your health, too much protein is hard on your body and may be linked to kidney and other organ damage.

Sometimes risky behaviors associated with fitness obsession have less to do with a desire to lose weight or change one's appearance than they have to do with other complicated situations in a person's life. Sometimes a fitness obsession can even be a symptom of a serious psychiatric disorder. Here are a few disorders that can be part of or can trigger a fitness obsession.

Body Dysmorphic Disorder

At one time or another almost everyone feels some dissatisfaction with at least one part of her body. For a period of time, that body part may occupy the person's thoughts, cause worry, and trigger unhappiness. A person with a healthy body image and a healthy self-image, however, will eventually come to accept the body part she had previously regarded as flawed. When you have a healthy body image, you realize that everyone's body is different, no one's body is perfect, and in fact the things that make a person's body different can be part of a person's beauty.

Sometimes, however, a person cannot accept a part of his body that he perceives as flawed. Continual unhappiness or dissatisfaction with a part of one's body will almost certainly have a negative effect on one's body image. Such persistent, negative feelings about a part of one's body can in rare cases escalate to a psychiatric disorder known as body dysmorphic disorder (BDD). A person with BDD focuses excessively on a part of the body that he perceives as flawed. Often, the body flaw is actually imagined, and yet the person cannot be convinced of his body's true state.

Not every person who worries about part of her body has a psychiatric disorder. If so, we would all be diagnosed with these disorders! To be diagnosed as having BDD, the focus on the body part must be so severe that it significantly impacts the person's life and impairs her ability to function normally. Furthermore, if a person's body obsession is related to or part of a different physical or psychiatric disorder, then the person would not be diagnosed as having BDD.

A person with BDD does not see her body part as simply flawed, but begins to regard even the slightest irregularities as serious deformities. This preoccupation with her perceived deformities can dominate all other considerations in her life. She will begin to think that other people are as preoccupied with her "deformities" as she is. Perhaps she will think that other people are always looking at her, talking about her, or laughing at her "ugliness." Her social interactions and relationships will suffer, and she may even become *delusional* about her body.

The most common body parts that people with BDD focus on are characteristics of the head or face, specifically the shape of the nose, mouth, teeth, eyes, and eyebrows or scars, wrinkles, and hair loss. It is also common for a woman to focus on her breasts, genitals, and hips and for a man to focus on the size or function of his penis. Not surprisingly, BDD occurs more commonly in image-oriented North America than in parts of the world that do not have such a powerful media. Perhaps surprising, however, is the fact that, at least in North America, men and women appear to suffer from BDD in roughly equal numbers. Onset of the disorder is usually between the ages of fourteen and twenty.

If a person with BDD perceives her weight as part of her "flaw," a fitness obsession could certainly result. No matter how much one exercises, however, if the root of the problem is a medical condition like BDD, no amount of exercise will help. No matter how much weight or how many inches the person loses, she will still see herself as flawed. This is because she cannot see the true reality of her body. In essence, it makes no difference what her body looks like because the only way she can see her body is as ugly or

flawed. These flaws, however, are largely in her mind. Even if her body does have a true physical irregularity that could be perceived as a flaw, the seriousness of that regularity is misconstrued by her mind. Simply "fixing" the body part will not cure the person of her body woes. She needs assistance from a professional, like a doctor, psychiatrist, or therapist, who can treat the issues that are more than skin-deep.

Anorexia Nervosa

Another psychiatric disorder that may involve fitness obsession as a symptom is anorexia nervosa. The most defining characteristics of anorexia nervosa, however, are self-starvation and extreme, often rapid weight loss. As with BDD, people with anorexia nervosa tend to have a distorted perception of their body's size and appearance. People with this condition will severely limit their food intake and often engage in excessive amounts of exercise to burn off any Calories they do take in. If a person has anorexia nervosa, she may also display intense fear of gaining weight or even a fear of food.

The health risks of anorexia nervosa are extremely serious. If untreated, this condition can cause permanent damage to the body and even death. Some of the most common effects of anorexia nervosa are fatigue; bad breath; weakening of the bones; dehydration; kidney damage; muscle loss; heart damage; hair loss; *cessation* of menstruation in women; and growing a layer of fine, downy hair all over the body (an attempt by the emaciated body to stay warm). Many people think that anorexia nervosa only affects girls and women, but this is untrue. Girls and women do experience anorexia nervosa at a far greater rate, but boys and men are increasingly presenting with the disease. The condition most commonly develops in the early teenage years. Like BDD, the poor body image that people with anorexia nervosa have cannot be cured by exercising more and losing weight. Medical treatment is needed.

> **Between five and twenty of every one hundred people suffering from anorexia nervosa will lose their lives to the disease.**

Bulimia Nervosa

Bulimia nervosa is another serious and relatively common eating disorder that is related to a distorted body image. Although a fitness obsession is unlikely to be a *cause* of bulimia nervosa, it can be a *symptom* or one tactic sufferers use to try to combat the illness.

As with anorexia, people with bulimia also tend to believe they are overweight and feel intense fear of food, fat, and weight gain. However, whereas in anorexia the defining characteristics are self-starvation and weight loss, the defining characteristic of bulimia is a pattern of bingeing usually followed by purging.

When a person binges on food, he consumes a huge amount of food in a very short space of time. During a bingeing event, he might consume five times the amount of food he would otherwise eat in an entire day. The person bingeing appears to lose control during these events and finds himself unable to stop the compulsive eating. When the bingeing ends, however, the person feels extreme remorse and depression. Sickened by his own behavior or frightened of the weight he will gain from the excessive caloric intake, he then endeavors to rid his body of everything he consumed. To accomplish this, he may force himself to vomit, take laxatives, engage in extremely

strenuous exercise, or abuse diet pills. A person with bulimia generally recognizes that his bingeing and purging pattern is abnormal and out of control, yet he feels powerless to stop it.

People with bulimia nervosa do not tend to have the same weight loss or emaciation that commonly accompanies anorexia nervosa. A person can suffer with bulimia for years yet never appear sick or too thin to her family and friends. Nevertheless, like anorexia nervosa, bulimia is a dangerous condition that can permanently alter one's health and even cause death. Some of the side effects of bulimia include damaged teeth, bad breath, burned esophagus, irritated lungs, dehydration, muscle weakness, seizures, and kidney damage. The most common cause of death among people with bulimia is heart failure due to a *depletion* of minerals like potassium and sodium. In bulimia nervosa, death is often sudden and completely unexpected. Like anorexia nervosa, bulimia occurs far more commonly among women, but rates appear to be rising among men. Also like anorexia nervosa, the distorted body images, depression, and persistent negative feelings that people with bulimia suffer from cannot be fixed by simply losing weight or becoming fit. These issues need to be addressed by trained medical professionals.

The risks we have discussed in this chapter, though serious and even frightening, are not brought on by a desire to be healthier or even a simple desire to look better. Usually they have serious underlying psychological causes. Nevertheless, in our highly image-conscious society, it is important for you to understand what some of the risks associated with a fitness obsession might be. You need to exercise to be healthy, but you also need to be in control. As with so many things in life, moderation and a realistic outlook are key.

Chapter 7

You Don't Have to Be an Olympic Athlete

- Starting Out

- For the Pleasure of It

- Don't Forget About a Healthy Diet

As you can see, striking a healthy balance in your life can be complicated. On the one hand, overweight and obesity are serious risks to your health. On the other hand, we all need to learn to accept our bodies without giving in to societal pressures to be ridiculously thin. Though the human body is made to move, and you need to have a certain amount of physical activity every day

to be healthy, you are a busy person with many important demands on your energy and time. But remember this: The health complications that come with overweight and obesity do kill, and you'll have many more years to do all those important things if you keep your body healthy.

Starting Out

None of this means, however, that you have to be an Olympic athlete. In fact, you don't have to be an athlete at all. We all can do things every day to add exercise to our lives and make ourselves healthier. Whether that means taking up running, bicycling to school or work instead of riding in a car, going for a walk after dinner, turning off the television and playing a game instead, or even doing some stretches while watching your favorite television show, there are lots of ways—both big and small—to add more activity to your life. And you don't have to begin by joining an expensive gym or doing an hour of vigorous exercise daily. If it's been a long time since exercise was a part of your life, then start out slowly. Anything is better than nothing, and doing just a little bit at first until your body gets stronger will help minimize the risk of injury, keep you from getting overly exhausted or frustrated, and steadily build your confidence.

We all can do things every day to add exercise to our lives and make ourselves healthier.

For the Pleasure of It

Perhaps the most important thing to remember is that exercise can and should be fun. If you just can't seem to get healthy because you find exercise a horrible, painful, exhausting drag, maybe you need to look for a different activity. If you're a person who loves being outdoors, don't try to make yourself run on a treadmill every day. Think of things you can do outside like hiking, camping, gardening, bicycling, skiing, horseback riding, and numerous other activities. If you, however, love television and dread the great outdoors, maybe exercise equipment set up in front of a television is right for you. If you're a person who lacks motivation, join an exercise group or start your own. Groups help keep each other motivated, and friends make exercise more fun. If starting your own exercise group, you may want to look for people who have a similar fitness level to your own. This way you and your friends can build your fitness level together. You won't have to feel intimidated around each other, and one of you won't be leaving the other in her dust.

Don't Forget About a Healthy Diet

While you're thinking about the importance of exercise and how to add it to your life, take a moment to consider your diet as well. Although when it comes to overweight and obesity, many people today focus too much on diet and not enough on exercise. What you eat is still an extremely important factor in your health. You need to give your body the right type of fuel if you're going to be exercising, and that means getting the right amount of Calories as well as nutrients from healthy sources like fruits and vegetables.

> "Success is not final. Failure is not fatal. It is the courage to continue that counts."
> —Winston Churchill

There's no denying it. Being overweight and obese have created a health crisis of epidemic proportions. These conditions and the health risks associated with them are not going to disappear overnight. Overweight and obesity develop over time, and they take time to reverse as well. Eating right and exercising daily are not easy, but they can be done. Furthermore, if a person finds he or she really cannot make the necessary lifestyle changes alone, more and more resources—from fitness facilities to doctors' offices—can help.

Overweight and obesity, though widespread, do not affect all Americans. The unhealthy American lifestyle, however, touches all of us. Now more than ever, it is important for us to realize that fitness is for everyone—and the fitness factor may be the most important link to developing good health.

Glossary

accomplices: People who knowingly help someone commit a crime.

alarmist: Unneccesary fear or warnings of danger.

arthritis: A disease characterized by a stiffening of the joints, pain, and swelling.

cardiovascular: Relating to the heart and blood vessels.

cessation: A stop, pause, or interruption.

coalesced: Merged into a single body.

delusional: Having persistent false beliefs in spite of evidence to the contrary.

depletion: The act of emptying or using up something.

disposable income: Income that remains after taxes and other obligations are paid.

entrees: Dishes served as the main part of the meal.

epidemic: An outbreak of a disease or condition that spreads more rapidly and more extensively than expected.

exploit: To take unfair advantage of someone.

foraging: Searching for food or supplies.

formidable: Inspiring respect or wonder because of size, strength, or ability.

genetics: Relating to, caused by, or passed on by genes.

inaccessible: Unable to be reached or attained.

industrialized: Focused on industry.

ingratiated: Gained favor or acceptance through a deliberate effort.

mantras: Repetitive chants.

media: The means by which information is transmitted, including television, radio, Internet, and newspapers.

metabolizes: Enacts the chemical changes in living cells by which energy is provided for vital activities and new material is made.

musculoskeletal: Involving both the musculature and the skeleton.

paradox: Something that appears to be contradictory but which may in fact be true.

permeates: Spreads or passes through something.

quotas: Fixed numbers that must be reached in order to receive something.

respiratory: Referring to breathing or the method by which an organism takes in and distributes oxygen.

sedentary: Not physically active; requiring much sitting.

self-esteem: Confidence in and satisfaction with oneself.

service-based economy: An economic system based on providing services rather than making products.

stereotype: A judgment based on incomplete and often inaccurate information.

stigma: The shame or disgrace attached to something socially unacceptable.

stipulate: To specify something as a condition or requirement of an offer.

triglyceride: A chemical compound formed from glycerol and molecules of fatty acids.

undermines: Weakens seriously.

Western: Typical of countries with cultures rooted in Greek and Roman traditions.

Further Reading

Berg, Frances M. *Underage and Overweight: America's Childhood Obesity Epidemic—What Every Parent Needs to Know*. Long Island City, N.Y.: Hatherleigh Press, 2004.

Brownell, Kelly D. and Katherine Battle Horgen. *Food Fight: The Inside Story of the Food Industry, America's Obesity Crisis, and What We Can Do About It*. New York: McGraw-Hill, 2003.

Critser, Greg. *Fat Land: How Americans Became the Fattest People in the World*. New York: Mariner Books, 2004.

Douglas, Ann. *Body Talk: The Straight Facts on Fitness, Nutrition and Feeling Good About Yourself!* Toronto, Ont.: Maple Tree Press, 2002.

Gaede, Katrina, Alan Lachica, and Doug Werner. *Fitness Training for Girls: A Teen Girl's Guide to Resistance Training, Cardiovascular Conditioning and Nutrition*. San Diego, Calif.: Tracks Publishing, 2001.

Hovius, Christopher. *The Best You Can Be: A Teen's Guide to Fitness and Nutrition*. Broomall, Pa.: Mason Crest Publishers, 2005.

Kirgerger, Kimberly. *No Body's Perfect: Stories by Teens about Body Image, Self-Acceptance, and the Search for Identity*. New York: Scholastic Inc., 2003.

Luciano, Lynne. *Looking Good: Male Body Image in Modern America*. New York: Hill and Wang, 2001.

McCoy, Kathy and Charles Wibbelsman. *The Teenage Body Book*. New York: The Berkley Publishing Group, 1992.

Pipher, Mary. *Reviving Ophelia: Saving the Selves of Adolescent Girls*. New York: G. P. Putnam's Sons, 1994.

Pool, Robert. *Fat: Fighting the Obesity Epidemic*. New York: Oxford University Press, 2001.

Pope, Harrison G., Katharine A. Phillips, and Roberto Olivardia. *The Adonis Complex: The Secret Crisis of Male Body Obsession*. New York: The Free Press, 2000.

Salter, Charles A. *The Nutrition-Fitness Link*. Brookfield, Conn.: The Millbrook Press, 1993.

Schlosser, Eric. *Fast Food Nation: The Dark Side of the All-American Meal*. New York: HarperCollins Publishers Inc., 2002.

For More Information

American Council on Exercise
www.acefitness.org

American Dietetic Association
www.eatright.org

Food and Nutrition Information Center
www.nal.usda.gov/fnic

Harvard School of Public Health: Food Pyramids
www.hsph.harvard.edu/nutritionsource/pyramids.html

Health Canada
www.hc-sc.gc.ca

Mind on the Media
www.mindonthemedia.org

National Center for Chronic Disease Prevention and Health Promotion's
Information on Obesity
www.cdc.gov/nccdphp/dnpa/obesity/index.htm

The National Eating Disorders Association
www.nationaleatingdisorders.org

National Institutes of Health: Calculate Your Body Mass Index
http://nhlbisupport.com/bmi/bmicalc.htm

The President's Council of Physical Fitness and Sports
www.fitness.gov

United States Department of Agriculture: Food and Nutrition Information
www.nal.usda.gov/fnic/Fpyr/pyramid.html

United States Department of Health & Human Services: The Surgeon
General's Call to Action to Prevent and Decrease Overweight and Obesity
www.surgeongeneral.gov/topics/obesity/

Publisher's note:
The Web sites listed on these pages were active at the time of publication. The
publisher is not responsible for Web sites that have changed their addresses or
discontinued operation since the date of publication. The publisher will review
the Web sites and update the list upon each reprint.

Index

Picture Credits

Banana Stock: pp. 36, 87

Benjamin Stewart: pp. 8, 16, 26, 40, 50, 72, 90

Clipart.com: pp. 11, 18, 19, 30, 31 (top), 45 (top and bottom), 49, 52 (bottom), 66, 74, 84, 93

Hemera Images: pp. 10, 22, 32, 30 (bottom), 52 (top), 53, 55 (left and right), 58, 59, 61, 69, 77, 78, 88, 92

Image Source: pp. 20, 31 (bottom)

MK Bassett-Harvey: p. 6

PhotoDisc: pp. 24, 35, 39, 43, 47, 85, 95, 96

Photos.com: pp. 12, 22, 25, 63, 70, 75, 80, 83

Biographies

Autumn Libal received her degree from Smith College in Northampton, Massachusetts. A former water-aerobics instructor, she now dedicates herself exclusively to writing for young people. Other Mason Crest series she has contributed to include PSYCHIATRIC DISORDERS: DRUGS & PSYCHOLOGY FOR THE MIND AND BODY, YOUTH WITH SPECIAL NEEDS, and THE SCIENCE OF YOUTH AND WELL-BEING. She has also written health-related articles for *New Moon: The Magazine for Girls and Their Dreams*.

Dr. Victor F. Garcia is the co-director of the Comprehensive Weight Management Center at Cincinnati Children's Hospital Medical Center. He is a board member of Discover Health of Greater Cincinnati, a fellow of the American College of Surgeons, and a two-time winner of the Martin Luther King Humanitarian Award.